War Cry
on a Prayer Feather

Southern Ute scouting party, Los Pinos Agency, 1899

NANCY WOOD

War Cry on a Prayer Feather

PROSE AND POETRY OF THE UTE INDIANS

DOUBLEDAY & COMPANY, INC.
GARDEN CITY, NEW YORK 1979

Library of Congress Cataloging in Publication Data

Wood, Nancy C
War cry on a prayer feather.

1. Ute Indians—Poetry.   I. Title.
PS3573.0595W3   811'.5'4
ISBN 0-385-12884-3 Trade
ISBN 0-385-12885-1 Prebound
Library of Congress Catalog Card Number 77–76272

Credits

Photographs facing title page and on pp. xiv, 10, 16, 20, 22, 24, 28, 31, 42, 45, 48, 53, 54, 60, 66, 71, 72, 78, 82, 87, 88, 106, courtesy The Denver Public Library, Western History Department; pp. 7, 32, 37, 38, 56, 68, 104, courtesy Pikes Peak Regional Library District; pp. 15, 50, courtesy Library of Congress; pp. 18, 74, 80, 92, courtesy State Historical Society of Colorado; pp. 34, 59, 65, 77, 95, 96, courtesy Pioneers' Museum, Colorado Springs, Colorado.

"My friend, Inspector, you are a good man, but I don't want you to talk to us. We came from away over yonder to this land and we like it here. From the top of the mountains, streams are running both ways. The other side belongs to the white man. My friends came up here with me and there are not many of us left. Here in this land are our relatives and children, covered over with earth. That is what makes this land dear to us. It is not buckskin or deer's hide and we do not want to sell it or give it away. I have not two hearts, I have but one; I have not two mouths, I have but one. I am not going to talk any different. I am telling you the truth just as you say you are telling us the truth."

Ute Indian leader, probably Red Cap,
to government committee seeking to
open Northern Ute Reservation to white
settlement, Fort Duchesne, Utah, 1905

"The government in Washington is your best friend and does not wish to impose any hardship upon your people."

James McLaughlin, government negotiator
to Northern Utes, Fort Duchesne, Utah, 1905

War Cry
on a Prayer Feather

Warrior and his bride, Uintah Utes, Utah, 1871

Preface

Of all the Indian tribes to inhabit the western United States, perhaps least is known about the Ute Indians, who now occupy two sage- and cactus-covered reservations in southwestern Colorado and one in the eastern Utah desert. Today, nearly a hundred years after their disintegration, the Utes live quietly, and often bitterly, on their separate reservations, apart from the mainstream of Indian life, influencing Indian thought and activism hardly at all. Their numbers are few, their lands sparse, their outlook a cross between communal integrity and common despair.

The Utes are juxtaposed between what the American public thinks they ought to be (wise and noble savages) and what their own inner conflicts tell them they are destined to become (unwise and ignoble white men). Deprived of the vast western lands that were theirs for centuries, the Utes have been literally cut off from their mountain roots and hence their heritage. Like every other Indian tribe in America today, the Utes are trying to determine how—if at all—they fit into modern life and what their options are, all the while despising white euphemisms such as "assimilation," "acculturation," and "identity." They want to carve out a place for themselves, with a full set of rights and priorities, yet they are without motivation to do so. The federal government, under the guise of the Bureau of Indian Affairs, controls or influences nearly every aspect of their daily lives; moreover, the tribal councils themselves tend to give only token support to traditional values, shifting more and more to a white man's system of government and duality.

Politically, the Utes have little clout in either Colorado or Utah; indeed, they are virtually ignored by both state legislatures, as well as by the public school system, which refuses to include Ute history or culture in their curriculum. Significantly, there is no Ute representation in either Utah or Colorado government, because Ute population is less than one tenth of 1 per cent of the states' total. In Colorado, few residents even know there is an Indian tribe still left in the state. To them, "Ute" is just a three-letter word often found in crossword puzzles.

The three Ute tribes—Southern Ute, Mountain Ute, and Northern Ute—differ widely in terms of life style, lands, and politics, with the Southern Utes the most dynamic economically, culturally, and socially. The Southern Utes pride themselves on recent gains in natural resource development under the leadership of outspoken tribal chairman Leonard Burch, who frequently assails the bureaucracy with cries of "white tape" when promised programs are not delivered to him. Said he to a meeting of white leaders over water rights, "We Utes are sick and tired of being shoved around."

Under Burch, Chris Baker, and Julius Cloud, the Southern Utes have been able to build a huge tourist complex at their reservation town of Ignacio, which, although it steadily loses money, provides a much-needed community center for the 850 members of the tribe. Moreover, the Southern Utes have taken steps to introduce the nearly forgotten Ute language to their people and to keep them informed via a tribal radio station and newspaper. However, internal politics, tribal dissension, and personal strife are never discussed via the news media, causing many Southern Utes to complain that they still don't know what is really going on.

It is impossible to generalize about the Utes, for they differ greatly as individuals. On the surface, most Utes live like their white counterparts, with their dusty reservations looking like any lower-middle-class white community—there is nothing "Indian" about any of them except for the tipis erected for the benefit of white tourists. Utes dress like whites except for ceremonial occasions, when treasured buckskin is carefully removed from trunks and dressers, and ancient headdresses are taken out of storage. Few Ute men wear their hair in braids any more, nor are their children encouraged to do so. Except for the deeply religious Sun Dance held by the Southern Utes and the Northern Utes (the Ute Mountain tribe abandoned this ritual in 1976), there are no ceremonials to link the people to a spiritual life. At Ignacio, tribal council member Eddie Box comes as close to being a medicine man as the Southern Utes have seen in more than thirty years; he presides over the Bear and Sun dances and offers "spiritual advice" to those who ask him.

In all three tribes, alcoholism remains the major social problem, affecting the young in particular; it is estimated that alcoholism afflicts one Ute out of three—average age, sixteen. Directly related to this is the suicide rate, which in the Ute Mountain tribe alone is higher than anywhere else in the world. Ute children, many coming from broken homes, generally drop out of high school by tenth grade; fewer than 1 per cent have ever attained a college degree. The situation is worst in the Ute Mountain tribe, which decided to award a trust fund to its young when they reached the age of eighteen; for some this meant a tribal handout as high as fifteen thousand dollars, often squandered on heavily chromed trucks and automobiles. This giveaway came to an end in 1977, when the Ute Mountain tribe ran out of money.

Unemployment is high on all three reservations, and there is much drifting from tribe to tribe and out of tribal life entirely. Life goals become confused amid family and tribal strife, and pressure mounts to abandon what is left of the old ways and to join the white society, which surrounds the Indians. The Utes themselves often seem immobilized. As one young college-educated Ute put it, "I came back to help my people and found they didn't want it. I stayed anyway, because here is the only place where *I* can feel like an Indian."

Tribal leadership, despite certain hard-earned economic and social gains, nonetheless wavers between a kind of paternal dictatorship and a capitalistic urge to exploit the Utes' considerable natural resources in oil, gas, and uranium. Moreover, all the old leaders have died off, taking strong religious belief with them. One of these, the last Ute Mountain chief, Jack House, who died in 1972, was a fierce opponent of government interference all his life. Acerbic, autocratic, and hardheaded, House kept his people together for more than forty years but eventually lost his power over them when an exploitation-minded younger generation unseated him politically. With the death of House, whose Indian name means Hand That Stops the Sun, the Mountain Utes have become divided and suspicious, accusing one another of lying, stealing, and council corruption. Indeed, a 1977 federal investigation revealed the Ute Mountain treasury nearly a million dollars short.

Yet in all three tribes there are a few individuals left who still

3

observe the old ways and possess an inner strength that is inde-structible. They are moderns in the sense that they have jobs, drive cars, and live in houses, but it is their spirit which prevails and re-mains timeless. Because of these few, the Utes will probably sur-vive at least until Western civilization wipes them out entirely. Young and old, men and women alike form this backbone of Ute strength; they are as solid now as their counterparts were more than a century ago. It is for them that this book is written; it is because of them that it came to be written at all.

A deeper, more detailed look at the lives of the present-day Utes will appear later, as another book. For now, it is enough to pass along certain thoughts gained from friendship with the Utes over the past several years. Although the ideas are universal, the attitude reflects that of the traditional Ute caught up in the modern (coun-tertraditional) world. No attempt has been made to do more than in-terpret the basic Ute idea toward himself, his land, and his destiny.

Nancy Wood

A History

Formidable both as hunters and warriors, the Utes once occupied most of Colorado from the Rockies westward to the eastern third of Utah; their domain stretched from the southern border of Wyoming nearly as far south as Santa Fe, about 125,000 square miles in all. Their number has been estimated at forty-five hundred at the height of their population, around the year 1800. By contrast, the Sioux nation at the time was twenty-seven thousand, the Comanche tribe, ten thousand.

Nomads and hunters but seldom planters, except for sporadic crops of corn, beans, and squash, the Utes early in their history formed into seven bands. Each band lived in a certain region, under a powerful leader who led their hunting parties and raids. Assailed by the Plains Indians, who dared periodic raids against them, and hated by their traditional enemies, the Navajos, the Utes remained virtually indomitable. The mountains formed a natural protection which other tribes feared to invade; the Utes moreover had a deep and abiding affinity for the shining peaks, the clear, rushing streams, and the tall, thick forests. They roamed freely from one end of the mountains to the other, inhabiting the lush valleys and lowlands also.

So they lived for five hundred years, perhaps more. Archaeological evidence is scanty and tries to relate them to the Mesa Verde cliff dwellers, who deserted their habitat around 1300. The Utes do not care either way. Asked where they came from, they will tell about the wolf with the bag on his back which kept getting heavier and heavier. He put it down and all the people of the world spilled out, talking in various languages. They all went to their places on

5

earth, but the Ute people stayed where they were, near the mountains that were the source of all life to them.

Ute life began to change when the Spaniards appeared in what is now New Mexico, at the end of the sixteenth century, bringing horses and a whole new life style up the Rio Grande Valley. Horses became the single most valuable and most coveted possession of the Utes, and they measured their wealth by them. So indispensable were horses that the Utes would even trade their children for them. With horses, they were able to ride out onto the plains after buffalo, which became their principal resource, providing food, shelter, tools, and clothing. More aggressive and warlike than ever before, the Utes moved out of their mountain fastness into the villages of friend and foe alike, helping themselves to livestock, agricultural products, and captives held for ransom.

Ute lands were scarcely disturbed during the Spanish period, which lasted from 1598 to 1821. The Mexican occupation of the Southwest, from 1821 to 1848, saw old, Spanish land grants reactivated and new, Mexican ones thrown in. Millions of acres were claimed, and the Utes lost nearly all of their homeland in New Mexico and southern Colorado, if not to land grantees, then to American forts, which began to ring their rich and bounteous preserve.

Once gold was discovered in Colorado, in 1858, it took less than fifteen years to destroy the Utes' vast domain, stretching from mountaintop to mountaintop, encompassing the seven major rivers to flow out of them and millions of acres of pristine forest. Treaty after treaty between the federal government and tribal leaders was broken as new gold strikes were made, and the Utes were shoved farther and farther back into the mountains and eventually out of them. The Utes, with childlike trust and simplicity, believed the government would not take everything.

At one point, in 1879, following the killing of the self-righteous Indian agent Nathan Meeker, who had unsuccessfully tried to make farmers of them, a public campaign was launched to remove every last Ute from Colorado. The nation was hungry for land, and thousands of white settlers teemed westward, backed by a government that created instant laws to aid in the seizure of all Ute lands. The mountains had yielded vast treasures of gold and silver; cattle and sheep ranches soon covered what had been Ute hunting grounds; towns and cities sprang up almost overnight on old Ute

Ute Mountain Ute reservation, Towaoc, 1908

campgrounds; railroads pushed through all the passes that for centuries had served as Ute pathways; and finally, the Ute domain was gone forever.

By 1896, two bands of Colorado Utes had been banished to the Utah desert at gunpoint and another two had been shoved onto a small reservation south of Durango. These, the Southern Utes, had been talked into accepting individual allotments of 160 acres each. What was left of the reservation guaranteed to them forever by the U. S. Government, some half million acres in all, was then thrown open to white settlement. Much of the allotted land was subsequently sold to Anglos and Spanish for a pittance; even so, the tribe managed to hold some blocks of land in common trust. Today, the Southern Ute Reservation, some 305,000 acres in all, resembles a checkerboard, with the tribal council constantly trying to buy what it can to make one long, contiguous reservation along the Colorado-New Mexico border. This land includes none of the high mountains that were once part of the Ute heritage. Much of it is semiarid and covered with low forests of piñon and scrub oak; the Southern Utes fortunately hold water rights to the Pine River but are now struggling to save them from white control.

The one remaining band that was still defiant, under Chief Ignacio, in 1894, the Weeminuche, refused allotments and instead simply remained entrenched on a chunk of desolate, waterless reservation land at the base of Ute Mountain. This land, some of the worst in the entire Southwest, belonged to the Southern Utes but was eventually given to the Weeminuche band, which became known as the Ute Mountain Utes. Since then, their reservation has been increased, mostly through trade, to 567,377 acres in Colorado, Utah, and New Mexico, all of it considered worthless until deposits of oil, natural gas, and uranium were discovered on it, in the early 1950s.

About this same time, the United States Government was finally forced to pay the Utes $32 million for lands it had illegally seized the century before, and the money was divided among the three tribes. The settlement amounted to roughly fifty cents an acre for mountains, rivers, forests, and all.

8

Introduction

These were our mountains.

As far as the eye can see, from the great, snow-capped peaks rubbing against the sky to the broad valleys where the buffalo used to lie, this land was our land. These mountains, with their great herds of game and pure streams flowing everywhere, were home to us. We knew the trees as one brother knows another. We knew the rocks as friends. We knew the rivers for their strength. We knew the meadows for their richness. We knew the animals by name. And always we watched the sky from here so that we knew the changing path of the sun. From here, we could tell about the life of stars and moon. We could tell about the life of thunder and clouds and rain.

To us, these mountains gave all that was necessary for life. We could not live away from them. We could only live as part of the life that was happening here every day, in every season and every kind of weather. This was our birthplace, the home of our ancestors. When we were poor in spirit, these mountains nourished us. When we were tired, these mountains gave us a place to lie down. When we were in pain from earthly wounds, these mountains cured us. We walked these mountains and felt their firmness with our feet. We were made strong with every step we took.

The Ute people are as natural as water to these mountains. It has always been so. Because we came from here, a certain spirit is part of us also. It happened in this way:

The spirit life of all living things is to be found in the shadow, which is always left behind. The rocks, the trees, the little flowers and the grasses, the animals and the birds, the insects and the fishes,

9

the turtle and the snake, the clouds and, yes, even the rainbow, all these things have shadows created by the sun. This is the path by which the spirit life comes out; you can see it for yourself any time you choose.

At day's end the spirit life extends itself all across the land, for it is with the dying of the sun each day that the spirit comes out the strongest. Even the great peaks spread out their shadows to the east, covering the valleys below with the spirit life they have. This is why the shadow places have always been sacred to us. The secret of life is in the shadows and not in the open sun; to see anything at all, you must first look deeply into the shadow of a living thing.

At night, the spirit life goes back into the living tree, the rock, the mountain, the bird, the fish, the deer, the spider, the fly, the buffalo, the sheep, the thrush, and so forth. Nighttime is a time of rest for body and spirit also; nighttime is when the spirits of the dead move around, and that is why we are always home in bed at night.

In the morning the spirit life comes out of every living thing again, commanded as it is by the sun. Nothing can move or change it, not even the powerful wind, which can move anything but cannot move a shadow so much as a hair. On cloudy days, when the sun is hiding, the spirit life hides also. For us, a cloudy day was always a time to be alone with our own spirits, for we left no shadows behind.

We found the spirit life strong within us as we walked along making a strong shadow. In the middle of the day it was very small, growing tallest when the sun was ready to go to sleep. When the sun rested, we rested also.

Now, when horses came, we moved through the mountains much faster; we were able to hunt the game with ease. We fought our enemies and beat them, for none were faster or better with horses than we were. No other tribe knew the mountains as well as we did, either. When horses came, the shadows moved much faster and we did not always take the time to look at them. We were in a hurry to be moving on. To us, the shadow of the horse was the spirit of his great ability. The horse was not sacred to us, like the buffalo; the horse was fast and beautiful. It was the horse which gave us wings.

In just a few short years we lost these mountains. The white man came and took them away from us. He found gold in them, and that

11

Butcher Jim, Southern Ute

was why he came. Gold was not important to us; it could not buy anything we needed. Gold did not cast a shadow either, and so there was no spirit to it. The white man divided us up. Some of our people were forced into the desert, others were forced into this, the southwestern part of the state and told to become farmers. We never did. Still others of us went to that dry and dusty mountain over there; many of us starved; many of us died of a broken heart. The white man never asked us what we wanted. If he had, we would have said: We want to stay in the mountains. We want to stay with the horses. We want to be watching the shadows for a sign.

What has come with us and is passed from one generation to the other is the imprint of those mountains on our minds. We lived there for so long that in our bones is the rock itself; in our blood is the river; our skin contains the shadow of every living thing we ever came across. This was what we brought with us long ago, along with certain friends we had.

The eagle with his majestic wings, the eagle came with us.

The bear, who long ago introduced us to one another, the bear came with us.

The deer we killed because we had to, the deer came with us.

The little spider who toiled so hard to catch the fly, the spider came with us.

The buffalo, who stood on the mountaintop and showed us where to go, the buffalo came with us.

There were tall grasses which blew in the winds of our minds. There were deep valleys which rolled out from the distance of our eyes. And the high places themselves, far above the trees where nature is always in battle, the high places came with us too.

Even now, after so many years, we can tell you what is happening there, for we have left our ancestors in the rocks. You can see their faces everywhere you look. The ancestors are watching over those mountains for us. Someday they will tell us when to go back.

We have always known certain things about the mountains. We can tell you about the agony of the wind, which cannot decide which way it wants to blow. We can tell you how Old Man Winter creeps down from the north when the forests are golden and lies down along the mountaintops, covering them with his white body, squeezing the streams shut with his icy fingers, blowing the clouds around with his strong breath. We can tell you about the turtle,

12

with his head to the north and his tail to the south, with his legs showing the direction of the summer and winter suns rising and setting. We can tell you about the sacred white buffalo, still standing on the mountaintop, breaking it open with his powerful hoofs so that the fire pours out and all the people are released. We can tell you about our Father, the sun, who is still creating shadows for the world to believe in.

We have not forgotten these mountains, which you tell us are now your own for you have built your cities and towns upon them; you have divided them up with fences and with roads; you have put tunnels through them; you have strung them with wires and put signs where you wanted to. The mountains are helpless against all that you have done to them; they quietly endure your punishment.

We say to you that the mountains are still our home. We can go there whenever we like, for they are all within us and always have been. We can find the shadow of the rock and tree and buffalo; we can go inside ourselves on cloudy days the way we used to. We believe in mountains, even if we do not believe in the God you gave us. We believe the mountains will become whole again and that we as a people will become whole also.

Not even you white people can crush the mountains. You cannot crush us as a people, either. Our shadows are too strong.

In the beginning my people were one people.
They were made of feathers and corn.
They were made of dust and bone.
My people rode the tail of the sun
And swung on a rope through the sky.
My people lived inside the earth
On water running backwards into time.

My people were one people.
The earth was one earth.
Then men without faces came
To offend the earth with lines.
     The rivers ran with fire
     The oceans roared with flame
     The mountains broke and crumbled
     And the wounded earth cried out.
My people turned to the angry sky
And prayed to the sorrowing moon
And to the stars deserting the night.
They prayed to the howling sun.
     But the sun gave up and died.

Ute warrior, circa 1885

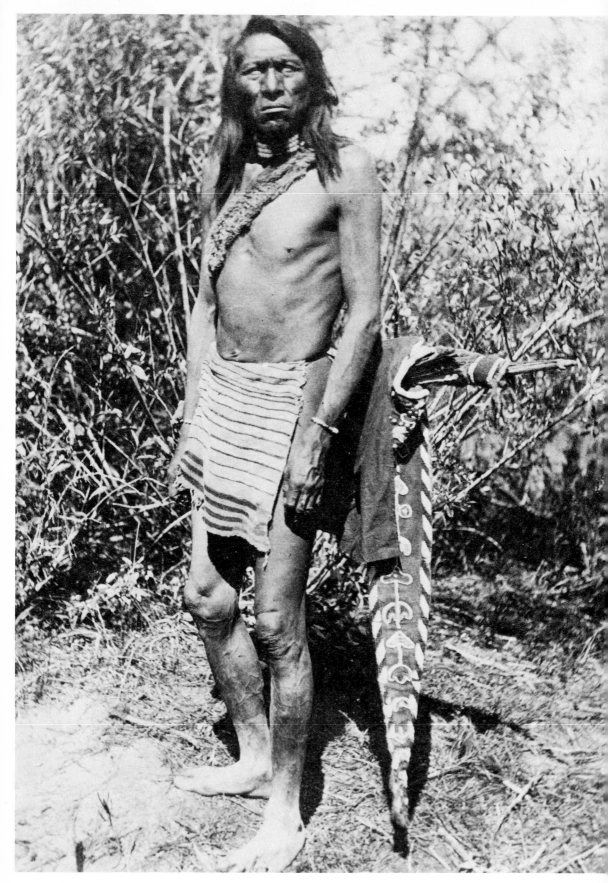

Pah-ri-ats, Uintah Ute, Utah, 1871

In the days when there were no days
And the nights were not counted yet
There were these Generations:

The Grandfather who created us
Drew his breath from the sun's energy
Then placed his lips upon the seed
Of birds, of animals, of man.

The Grandmother issued stars and moon
From her breast of sacred light,
Offered the mystery of sky
And the healing robe of night.

The Father, who is the living sun,
Scattered darkness before him
Then announced the growth of root and bone
With the coming of each dawn.

The Mother became the enduring Earth.
Naming Wind and Fire and Water,
She gave life to generations
And harmony to stones.

The Children passed from the hands of parents,
Gathered up root and bone,
Embraced the world with laughter

Then showed the Grandfather in.

Piah, left, *chief of the Tabeguache band, and warrior*

In the highest heaven, the Sun God lives, creating all that was ever created. This is the Great Spirit, the Supreme One, who shows the way. The Sun has a female part, which stretches out and is called the Earth. It has a male part, which arches over and is called the Sky. The Sun God is perfect unity. All life flows from this one source and we worship it every day.

Under the One Great Spirit, we believe there are Five Lesser Spirits. Through them the Sun God tells us what to do.

There is the Spirit of War, which is with us when we go out to fight our enemies. This is a Spirit of Protection and Vitality. We find this Spirit in the Eagle, who flies over us as we go.

There is the Spirit of Peace, which is with us always. Through this Spirit we live for the day when the earth will be green again, when there will be plants and animals as before, and when our ancestors will again be with us.

At first there was nothing but water, and the Spirit of Floods came out of it. Land came out of the water and people came out of the land. Some of them were bad people, and so the Spirit of Floods came and destroyed everything. This is the Spirit of Cleansing and Rebirth, sent by the One Above to remind us that the waters will come again.

There is the Spirit of Thunder and Lightning, which comes to tell us when it is spring. This is the Spirit of Promise and Uplifting. This Spirit is a messenger telling us to awake and spread out in all directions after a long winter together. The Spirit of Thunder and Lightning brings the rain, which comes to scatter seeds and make rivers.

Uintah Ute children, Wasatch Mountains, Utah, 1871

There is the Spirit of Blood, to heal the sick. When we warriors were wounded in battle, we always called upon this spirit to keep us from dying in front of our enemies. When women gave birth to children, they always called upon the Spirit of Blood to heal them and help make the children strong. All through life, the Spirit of Blood keeps us alive and well. In the old days, we did not die from diseases that other tribes had.

All these spirits work together for the benefit of our people. They have power, yes, but the true power is with the Great Spirit, the Sun. It has always been so among us.

We shall endure for there is
    no other way than endurance.
We shall accept pain for there is
    a lesson to learn in suffering.
We shall learn to think for ourselves
    for our minds are waiting to be heard.
We shall honor peace when it comes
    for we have been too comfortable with war.
We shall call upon our enemies
    for in them are our brothers born.
We shall overcome our weakness
    when our strengths have all come home.

Veeminuche encampment, Towaoc, 1884

Ute warrior

We can only make our own waves
     our own warmth
     our own light.
Loyal to the wave, one is drowned
     at the level.
Yielding to the warmth, one is consumed
     by the fire.
Lending importance to light, one is condemned
     to the dark.
After death, silence.
Speak now and watch the others stare.
Say nothing and listen to your own despair.

Our grandfathers told us we were a brave people.
Our grandfathers told us we were known for our bravery once.
Our grandfathers told us never to let go.

Our fathers told us we lost our braveness when the white man came.
Our fathers told us we were people who were no longer brave.
Our fathers told us to forget about what used to be.

Our children ask, Were we a brave people once?
We say, Yes, but we do not remember it.
Our children ask, What happened when the white man came?
We say, It happened a long time ago.
Our children ask, Are we a brave people still?
We say, We believe it to be so.

Our children ask, Why do you believe it to be so?
We say: We are able to live with the cat
even though we are all mice.
We are able to lie down with the lion
even when they are calling us sheep.
Like a snake we are able to swallow our own tail.
Like a gopher we are able to stay out of sight.

There is no way to live peacefully among you
When the order of life is judged as inefficient
And knowing oneself is termed impractical,
Leaving obedience to the popular front.
The moment is claimed by aliens insisting
That proof of victory lies in silence
And that the shame of invasion
Is borne by a single generation only.
Why should I explain myself in random words
Falling as you would have them?
Why should I justify my small path invisible
To your eyes clouded with roads to glory?
Why should I presume to tell you
What requires a lifetime of definition?
For me it is enough to bear the fruit
Of solitary confrontation:
Reason is situated between doubt and evasion.
Argument becomes inevitable comparison.
Bitterness results from inequality.
Firmness arises from knowing one's place.
Wisdom is the yield of contemplation.
Fear is lost before courage finds it.
Love matters most when mortality denies it.
Death is the failure of life to arm itself.
Indifference triumphs when effort crumbles
And nature must pause to refresh itself.
Like one who is blind and sees nonetheless
Darkness responds to my quietness.

Southern Ute scouting party, Los Pinos River, 1899

We had this land for ten thousand years.
Ten thousand summers of rejoicing.
Ten thousand winters of sleeping.
Ten thousand autumns of hunting.
Ten thousand springs of awakening.
Now this land is but a memory
    of inherited memories.
This land is just a story
    of repeated stories.
We do not know for ourselves
    the fullness of these mountains.
We only know the ache of it.
We have not slept on unblemished earth.
We only feel what we are able to imagine.
Now this land is filled with monuments
    to this man's cleverness
    and that man's dishonesty.
The land is worn out and sick.
Even now, they fight to divide it even more.
We would not welcome the return
    of these mountains to us.
We would not desire to know the freshness
    of what is leftover air.
Now we must go and keep on going
Toward our unknown destination
    to a sun that has not set
    to a moon that is not risen.

Earth teach me stillness
As the grasses are stilled with light.
Earth teach me suffering
As old stones suffer with memory.
Earth teach me humility
As blossoms are humble with beginning.
Earth teach me caring
As the mother who secures her young.
Earth teach me courage
As the tree which stands all alone.
Earth teach me limitation
As the ant who crawls on the ground.
Earth teach me freedom
As the eagle who soars in the sky.
Earth teach me resignation
As the leaves which die in the fall.
Earth teach me regeneration
As the seed which rises in spring.
Earth teach me to forget myself
As melted snow forgets its life.
Earth teach me to remember kindness
As dry fields weep with rain.

To-wee, wife of Chief Buckskin Charley, Capote band, 189

Southern Ute family, 1890

There is a danger to work
Dividing being and doing
Confusing lesson and learning
Isolating growth from pain
Separating thought from experience
Mixing loneliness with expectation
Quenching thirst with passion
Satisfying hunger with gain.
Work is the excuse of the unworthy.
The unworthy are the tools of ambitious men.
Ambitious men stem from an ambitious nation.
An ambitious nation drifts in one direction
Mistaking it for aim.

Shavano, chief of the Uncompahgre Utes, 1898

To live one must make a living.
In making a living we lose our faces
And see instead the images
Of what we have become.
If only
If only
Life did not become a business.

A UTE PRAYER FOR FRIENDSHIP

I greet the highest in you.
Your goodness walks in front of me.
Your gentleness bids me good day.
Your laughter raises me to joyfulness.
Your quietness leads me away.

Ute ceremonial

Setting tepee poles, 1894

We have forgotten our old ways.
The hoofs of the buffalo pound across
the empty spaces of our minds.
The language of our fathers rests
with old voices beneath the ground.
The dances of our warriors seeking strength
have risen on the dust and blown away.
Even the names we had to show our place in nature
remain unspoken.
Who among us will answer to them?
We have forgotten our old ways.
The homes we made of sticks and hides
are remembered by what they tell us.
The long winters and the search for meat
have been erased by what lies upon our plate.
Our old horizon stretching as far as one day's ride
has been shortened by the endlessness of the road.
Even the clouds do not appear as messengers any more
And the wind carries no secrets with it.
Our spirits are drowned in rain that never comes.
Our hopes lie still in the dust that covers our minds.
Our bodies sag from the weight of so much pride.
We have forgotten our old ways.

FIVE LEGENDS

Never leave the doors and windows of your house open. If you do, a bird will fly in, and then it is too late. Somebody in your family will die. There is nothing you can do to prevent it.

For us, to comb our hair at night brings evil. To sweep the floor at night brings evil also. If we go about whistling at night, the coyote will come and attack us. Our grandfathers taught us this. It must be so.

The Water Baby lives in the river down there. If you children stay out at night, he will catch you and eat you. The Water Baby has a big mouth and a mustache. He has long black hair that floats in the water after him. If you listen carefully, sometimes you can hear the Water Baby crying at night because he has no little children to eat.

This is the way we remember it. In the old days we covered our mirrors with animal hides during a thunderstorm. We also threw our dogs outside. Dogs and mirrors attract lightning and we were afraid we would be killed.

In the old days, an animal would make several conditions before giving its body to us for food. One was that nothing be wasted, not even the bones, which we kept away from dogs and menstruating women. Another condition was that we kill no more than what we needed. If we did not do this, the animals would make themselves scarce and we would starve.

"We have become so much like you whites that we have had to learn a whole new vocabulary to tell about it."

Chief Jack House   1962
Ute Mountain Ute Tribe

bonus	liberty	board of directors
payroll		
schedule	criminal	draft
commute	jury	Army
work week	Bill of Rights	Infantry
compensation	tourist	honorable discharge
fringe benefit	vacation	revolution
expense account	sight-seeing	court-martial
deduction	strike	sin
promotion	quit	damnation
boss	union	martyr
employee	bargain	apostles
standard of living	production	Jesus Christ
class		
success	assembly line	Virgin Mary
failure	efficiency	Holy Ghost
salary	bureaucracy	salvation
raise	expert	Pope
Social Security	official	saints
retirement plan		
nursing home	paper work	penance
welfare	document	heaven
minority	red tape	hell

41

Ignacio, chief of the Weeminuche band, 1898

integration
discrimination
prosecution
evidence
liability
asset
career
market
real estate

private property

public domain
wilderness
contract
license
buy/sell
lease
ownership
loan
interest
bankrupt
investment

profit
suburban
credit
appraisal
homestead
compass

fence
survey
title
acre
county

boondoggle
progress report
budget
responsibility
task-force report
mayor
election
transportation
wheels

stairway

inauguration

President
Congress
department
committee
lobby
fiscal year
taxes
chairman
Declaration of
    Independence
amendment
ambassador
administration
subsidy
inspection
assassin
accounting office
short check
computer
credit card

space program
politics
system
competition
bargain
credentials
aptitude
qualification
job description
style
advertisement
fashion
hospital

insurance
mail order
catalogue
status quo
protest
motivation
stock market
demonstration
liberation
civil rights
equality
objective
depression
guilt
neurotic
game warden
sheriff
evangelist
pilgrim
anthropologist
sociologist

When you white people came, you tried to take everything away. Our land first. Then our children, to be educated. You dressed us in leftover clothing sent by missionaries from the East. You gave us names you picked out, and told us not to use our Indian names. You would not let us use the language we knew, and beat us when we spoke it. You told us we were too incompetent to run our lives, but we were competent enough to sign our names to your papers. You took away our rights to hunt game and feed our families ourselves. You made us dependent on you for the bread that filled our stomachs. You brought the missionaries in and told us not to practice our Indian religion. You would not let us sing our songs or dance our dances. You called us pagans and savages, wards of the government, children of the Great White Father.

You never called us men and women, brothers and sisters. You gave us orders to farm, even though we were not farmers. You would not let us visit our sacred mountains for a long time, and then you told us we had to have a pass. You made us live in the desert, scattered us like leaves, separated us from our families, gathered us up only to tell us about some new treaty to scatter us even more.

When all was said and done, you told us that we Indian people were now just like you whites. You told us that we were to be thankful for it.

Now it is beginning to change. You come here and wonder where our feathered headdresses are. You want to see us in buckskin and beads. You would like to see us on horses, chasing the buffalo once again. You would be happy if we lived in tipis and used bows and

Group of warriors, 1894

arrows. You want us to sing and dance the way we used to. You want us to teach you our old ways so that you can write about them. You are writing down our language in order to teach it back to us. You ask, What is your Indian name?

White man, we say to you: Where is your covered wagon? Where is your musket? Where are your women in bonnets and long skirts? Where are your houses made of logs? Where are the soldiers who used to chase us? Where are the horses we loved so well? Where have the buffalo gone?

White man, can't you see that we're getting more like you every day? Only a few of us hold to the Indian way. Long ago, when you were taking everything from us, you did not take the sacred knowledge that we have. That is all we have left of what we used to be; it is all we will need when the time comes. For we are running out of earth and sky and water; we are running out of grass and meat and grain. When the time comes, it is we Indian people who will know what to do.

> We as a people have been blown to the wind.
> We as a family have been able to endure.
> We as one or two have been able to stand together.
> We as the seed of future generations are careful to remain inside.

I wish the quiet heart.
Forced to choose a separate world
I crawl in order to stand alone.
I wish the quiet heart.
An exile from my borrowed land
I search for a place to call home.
I wish the quiet heart.
I wish the quiet land.
All around me quiet.
All around me peaceful.
All around me lasting.
All around me home.

Uintah Ute boy in the Wasatch Mountains, Utah, 1871

Never probe into the Great Mystery.
It was meant to be that way.
It is the Great Mystery of Life that you must
    keep on securing
    keep on professing
    keep on defending.
Others will try to explain it to you.
They will say it has been proven.
They will expect you to believe them because
    religion has created respectability
    science has eliminated possibility
    education has elevated theory.
To master fate, one needs to apply reason.
To obtain happiness, one must avoid dilemma.
To examine life, one must strip away mystery.
    So they say.
In striving for the peak, one denies the valley.
    Why try so hard?
    True happiness is impractical.
    What can follow after?

Ute warrior and his bride

I give to you this life
    which is not the only life I have.
I am the forest living and dying.
I am the melancholy of falling leaves.
I am eternity in green.
I am water flowing strongly
Not in the lifetime of one man only
But down the rocks of generation
Across old deserts of humiliation
I run in anticipation toward the sea.
I give to you this life
    which is the outer garment only.
I have clothed myself in riches
Sewn by hands in praise of home.
I am made of pollen and wings and bone.
    I am wind reflected in moonlight.
    I am ice crying out for food.
    I am fire embedded in stone.
    I am fields released by sun.
I give to you this life
    claimed by what I do not own.

What is my life?
A family raised according to the way?
Words written according to conviction?
Action crippled by excuses?
Who will remember my children?
Who will consider my words?
Who can follow action never taken?
Did I live to be an example to others
Or to learn my limitation?
If that is so, then there is no answer.
The question is always arising.

Southern Ute family, 189

Buckskin Charley, chief of the Capote band, 1899

Be a warrior of small wars
Accustomed to small praise
For honesty and do not fight
For the sake of attainment.
Build a house of solid thoughts
A fortress of introspection
Feed and shelter all who enter
Protect and not possess them.

Warrior, Los Pinos Agency, 1899

I do not live here in the confusion
Of ready-made fire and
Quick wings mounted on rubber wheels.
I do not live here confined
By rectangular shapes and lines
Dividing me from people I used to know.
I do not live here behind
A door closing out tomorrow's sun
Allowing only disorder in.
I do not live here looking out
A window covered to keep me blind
To other men's despair.
I do not live here where I am known
As an address without a home
And a name which has
No person living in it.

I am two pieces of a whole split
For the sake of convenience into
What is perceived as obsolete and
What is proposed as advantage.
I am divided between a world I never knew
Yet believe to be a fruitful existence
And a world I know through experience is
A world which endangers the species.
I am caught between a sensible decision
And the vagueness of affirmation.
What affirmation amidst decay?
What possibility lies within
Impersonal reports of catastrophes
Internal reports of committees set up
For the conversion of natural law
Into a formula for easy dominion?
I am the convergence of illusion and delusion
Holding me to a thin line of stamina
While I become content with less
While growing less content with more.

*Ouray, chief of the Tabeguache band,
and Otto Mears, interpreter, 1880*

Ute Mountain Ute, circa 1897

Look up, the Old Man said, and tell me what you see.
    There are clouds, I said, in the shapes of buffalo.
    There are this year's blossoms growing out of last year's rain.
    There is a blackbird going by.
Look down, the Old Man said, and tell me what you see.
    There is green grass, I said, growing through dead leaves.
    There are last year's fruits and next year's seeds.
    There is a red spider going by.
You are confused by what you see, the Old Man said.
What lies above is vision.
What lies below is vision.
In between is where life joins
vision then to vision.
In between is where time draws the true dimension.
In between is not in between at all
But rather
The absence of it.
    The Old Man's words went around their meaning
    Perceived too much as reason.
    The more I look the less I see,
    I told the Old Man, crying.
    The less I see, the more I desire vision.
Good, the Old Man replied.
You do not need eyes for vision.
You do not need ears to understand.
You do not need a tongue to speak.
    What is necessary, then? I asked the Old Man kindly.
    But he was gone and in his place
    I felt my body growing.
    At last I touched both earth and sky
    And no longer asked for vision.

What remains beyond us to know
Is sought as meaning and reason
And the obsession to open the universe
Is excused as understanding nature.
In order to use life well
We must surrender our importance
And open ourselves to nature
To discover the universe there.

Be still until the waters clear.
Do nothing until the darkness ends.
Rest until the storm clouds pass.
Wait for winter's breath to die.
Nature does not fight against itself
Nor does it dance when the music ends.

All of my life rolled out from my feet
Which touched the earth
And danced to the drums in my heart.
I danced to the sun and the wind
And my head touched the clouds as
The rainbow ran through my eyes.
Fire fire house of dawn
Eagle lion feathers torn
Woman child man and dust
Buffalo bear one-eyed bird
Flowers dancing walking rain
Silent thunder lightning cold
Heart of shadows nest of bone
Fire fire feet and drums
I am the music I dance to everywhere.
I am the beat of time.

Southern Ute Bear Dance, 1898

Back row: *Ce-gie-che-ok, To-wee*; front row: *Tachiar,
A-pat-we-ma, and Tan-nah, Southern Utes,* 1899

Where is the woman I was yesterday
Gathering up footprints
To make the spirit come back?
Where are the words I spoke yesterday
Scattering thoughts around starlight
To prove the sky is mine?
Where are the steps I walked yesterday
Losing myself when darkness came
To better understand the light?
Where is the woman I was yesterday?
I do not recognize myself in last year's clothing.
I do not bend to last year's warning.
Where are the words I spoke yesterday?
I hear the echo of a language without memory.
I hear old songs repeated and voices waiting.
Where are the steps I walked yesterday?
I left a footprint without showing where I'd been.
I gathered up the trail behind me in order to see ahead.
Where is the shadow I left yesterday?
I gave my shadow to the child I'm constantly becoming.
I gave my spirit to generations already gone.
I saved my life to live sanely.
I gave my importance away.

To-wee and Buckskin Charley, chief of the Capote band, 1894

We have grown together you and I
Like two trees I saw once
Sharing a common root.
One tree gave shade,
The other light.
The trees grew strong and tall together.
They protected one another.
One tree was home to the other.
One tree was always looking out.
They endured the cold together.
They lived when there was no rain.
The trees shared sunlight and sky.
They shared earth and water.
The trees that I saw once
Grew together until at last
When winter came they died
And went back to the earth as one.

Keeper of my delight
Come rejoice with me.
Keeper of my sorrow
Come shed your tears with me.
Keeper of my drums
Come make a new song with me.
Keeper of my dreams
Come sleep a while with me.
Dance with me on rocks
Wet with springtime rain.
Lie with me on grass
Warm from summer sun.
Rest with me on leaves
Bathed in autumn light.
Walk with me through forests
Dressed in winter snow.
Keeper of my love
Keep my ambition for me.
Keeper of my heart
Keep my secrets to you.
Keeper of my home
Keep my fire for me.
Keeper of my garden
Keep its stillness for us.

Along Los Pinos River, Ignacio

He was a young man going out
To see what the world contained,
In his own way an explorer
Of the universe
Sailing a rudderless ship,
Taking the wind as it came
Blown back against the shore
Again and again he set out alone
To prove existence to himself.
He saw then the sea yielding and taking
And the passing of whole generations
Decreasing even as they became more
And nature reaping the decay of its harvest,
Understood the knowledge given on
The crest of a single wave
Poised for a moment before consuming
The vacancy before it.
He was a young man coming home
To listen to old stones growing
On a mountainside alone
And thus he learned
To live within himself on a landscape
Made of incomplete circles,
Owning nothing yet amassing wealth

Ta-wits-nan, 1899

Tree-house for the dead, made to speed their journey to the sky.
Uintah Utes, 1871

Doing nothing yet becoming a user of life,
Moving often yet leaving not a trace.
He was considered a fool
For his efforts which were alien to work
And his words which dimmed his meaning.
He lived his life to a ripe old age
Then left his lesson to be read:
I have no death to die, he said.

I see myself among the living
Who have all died
Without memory to their names.
My father and my daughter
Lie buried here beneath
Official lists of improbable facts
Listing cause of death
As defiance of the rules.
You never knew our names
Or how we lived
Among the coyotes and the buffalo
Taking courage from their eyes.
You only knew us
As an adversary
Victorious over your minds.

The earth is all that lasts.
On and on in loneliness
The dry earth cracks and opens
Bleeding dust and bones
Healing itself through time
Moving across its tortured skin.

Oh patient earth so restless
You are in weakness strong.
Within the mountain of your ashes
Lies the river of my fire.

Oh weeping earth reborn
With the death of living men
Let your strength flow into me
And my cry become your song.

The earth is all that lasts.
The earth is everywhere in me
Even when I'm gone.

Julian Buck and squaw, 18

Wich-ha-ka-sa, 1899

Because I spent the winter sleeping with a fish,
there is a fin within me now.
Because I spent the spring with an eagle in her nest,
there is an egg within me now.
Because I spent the summer with the buffalo,
there is a bone within me now.
Because I spent the autumn growing with one tall tree,
there is a root within me now.

I am but a footprint on the earth
A wing against the sky
A shadow in the water
A voice beneath the fire
I am one footstep going on.

Southern Ute, 1899

There are those who hear the voice of wheels
And call it music.
And those who hear a symphony
In butterfly wings.
There are those who ride a highway
And call it beauty.
And those who follow the straight line
Of a spider's silver thread.
There are those who define living
As existence only
And those who cannot live
Except to define existence first.
There are those who run in circles
And those who simply run
And those who find movement
In the greatest stillness.
Go one way or the other.
Fight for wheels or butterfly wings.
Travel on highways or spider threads.
Take up the cause of movement.
Bury stillness with the dead.
Abandon home for the popular place.
Kill the roots by girdling the tree.
Those who know the greatest comfort
Take not the greatest ease.
Those who prosper most
Prosper more with less.

Tab-u-cha-kat, Northern Ute

Some of us are lost, yes. Some of us are not even red any more. Some of us have become so white that we blind each other with our purity.

Some of us have given up, yes. Some of us do not have the strength to fight the white man any more. Some of us would be fighting ourselves.

In a strong forest there are always weak trees. There are trees that have given up. Maybe they cannot reach the light. Maybe they cannot reach the water. So they die because they cannot reach anything.

Do you think that because a tree stands in one spot all its life it is happy to be there? Do you think a tree gets tired of resisting the wind? Do you think a tree gets tired of cold and snow? Do you think a tree gets tired of always the same view in all directions?

That is how it is with some of our own people. They are tired of standing in one place forever, exposed to the harshest weather. They are tired of seeing the same view. They die because they cannot reach anything.

So it is that our people move on, away from this place, to a different soil and climate, to a different view entirely. They try to become birds of one feather, but they are always recognized as what they are.

How else could it be with people who have always been trees?

If the root is not clean
Nature will not bring forth a single flower.
If the earth is inhospitable to it
Nature will not bargain to come in.
If fruits of harvest rot in vengeance
Nature will imprison the seed.
But if all is made ready in reverence
Nature will nourish the land.

Do you hear the cry my memory makes
Now that it has deserted time?
Listen to the way the wind howls
And you will know
The sadness that is mine.

I would like to be a tree
    but you would cut me down.
I would like to be a river
    but you would build a dam.
I would like to be a bird
    but you would poison what I eat.
I would like to be a deer
    but you would shoot me for my meat.
I would like to be a fish
    but you would catch me in your net.
I would like to be a coyote
    but you would want me for my skin.
I would like to be a grizzly bear
    but you would kill me because I'm rare.
I would like to be a flower
    but you would pick me to take home.
I would like to be what I am.
    Is there any hope for that?

Piah, chief of the Tabeguache band, 189.

I am the woman who holds up the sky.
My feet are planted in all generations.
My roots go deep into melted rock.
I walk through darkest night
Wearing starlight in my hair.
I am the woman who holds up the sky.
The rainbow runs through my eyes.
The sun makes a path to my womb.
My thoughts are in the shape of clouds
But my words are yet to come.

Ra-de-da and Pio Pinos, Southern Utes, 1899

The earth is my shadow.
My shadow is formed of the earth.
The earth stills my heart within me.
My heart is reborn in the earth.
The earth leads me to my center.
My center is a shadow within me.
The earth is the substance within me.
The shadow of earth is within me.
The earth is the answer within me.
The answer is the substance of earth.

In the old days we had peace within ourselves.

Even in times of hardship, when game was scarce and winters cold, we had peace within ourselves. You may ask, how did we come by it? but I cannot give you an answer. I only know that we were born with the seed of peace within us. As we went through life, the seed grew and grew until it became like a solid tree within us. We could feel its branches filling up our veins; we could feel its sap within us. We could feel the roots it gave us, deeper and deeper all the time. No matter what happened, we were able to take it. We were able to show ourselves together even when we were only one.

The coming of the white man changed all this. In less than one man's lifetime we were destroyed. The peace within ourselves soon turned to bitterness and hate. Yet there was still this seed I am talking about. They did not kill the seed within us. But we did not know it at the time.

The way I remember it was this.

There was a young man who belonged to an old band and an old family. One day when he was sixteen or so his father decided it was time to send him away to learn something. So the young man went far beyond the mountains to where the white man was. The white man had not yet come West; he did not know what treasures lay in our mountains. He had no reason to hate us, but he hated us anyway; he hated us because we were so like our brothers in the East, who were making so much trouble. So when this young man went to live among the white people, they were afraid of him. They asked, What do you want from us?

They began to guard their women and children; they began to

Ute Indian children, 1894

lock up their houses so nothing would be stolen. What do you want from us? the white people asked again. The young man never said anything. This made the white people angry. They kicked the young man and beat him. They ran him out of the town where he was staying and told him they would kill him if he decided to come back.

The young man moved on, farther and farther East. He saw great cities where the buffalo had been. He saw smoke in the sky where his dreams began. He saw the great forests cut down; he heard the cry that trees make before they crash to the ground. He saw rivers that had dried up and lakes that were orange and green from the factories that were going up. The young man saw a terrible world out there, and at last he decided to come home.

Now, by this time we had already been driven out of the mountains, in the few short years that the young man had been gone. The young man's family had been killed by the troops who came to move us out. We had lost our homeland, which had been his homeland also; we had lost everything that was important, and we were broken by it. We had no will to get up and start over.

The young man had come back intending to tell how it was in the country where the white man lived, but when he saw us living as we were, huddled together and afraid, something came over him. He squatted down in the dirt where we were living in tents and eating whatever food the white man decided he could spare us. The young man looked around at the children who had not been born when he left. He saw children who had grown up while he was gone. He saw that they were still curious about things, and so he said:

I have been out across the great mountains to the east. I have crossed the great rivers that flow from them. I have slept in the great forests that cover them. I have killed deer and elk and buffalo; I have caught big fish in the streams. I have seen great beauty in the land.

The elders began to grumble and talk among themselves, for they knew that what the young man said was not true. They tried to stop him from talking, but he went on:

I have found peace out there among what is wild and free. I have found beauty, for I still have eyes to see. There is a world to be seen from the inside out. There is a world to be seen with the heart.

93

The young man talked all day and long into the night. He told his stories about things that we had nearly forgotten. The children listened to him until they began to fall asleep. Then their mothers took them away.

When the children were all in bed, the elders said: Why have you told us such lies? Why haven't you told about the sorrow the white man brings? Why have you done such a thing?

The young man said: I could have told of ugliness, for that is what everyone sees. I could have spoken of ugliness, for that is what everyone wants to hear. I could have told of such horror that no one would want to live any more. But I have said what I said for a purpose. I have said what I said so there is something for the children to believe in long after we are gone.

On that day the seed began to grow once again. The people began to feel it within themselves, and they passed it on to the children, and the children passed it on to their children. They are passing it on to this very day.

That is why we are able to show ourselves together even when we are only one.

Southern Ute brave, 18

Who speaks for animals who cannot talk?
Who sees for flowers which are blind?
Who guards the river which has but one course?
Who represents the mountain in time?
Who comes here to argue for the life of beavers?
Who will tell of the importance of snails?
Who has seen the mantis shed his skin?
Who believes in butterfly wings?
I am nature's advocate
Ten million birds
Ten million trees
Ten million animals
Ten million fish
Are mine.
I will fight you in this room
And out of it.
I will dare you to define
Progress
On the face of a dime.

97

We are all one.
The surface and the essence appear the same.
It is only words which make a difference.
Concealing wonder
Revealing shame
Expressing what cannot be expressed.
Existence remains between us
With surface and essence of equal claim.
It is up to you never to explain
But to keep to yourself
The knowledge that
There is more to fire than a flame.

We are land and sea
        earth and sky
You with roots cannot grow wings.
You with fins cannot grow feet.
But you with roots can recognize the bird
        for what he is.
And you with fins can see the bear
        for his life apart.
You can learn about what you are
        by observing what you are not.
That which is your opposite
        is what makes your shadow start.

Capitaneto, Chief Piah, Chief Severo, and Nachivera, 1894

A hundred years too late.
A hundred years too soon.
We move through life suspended
Between the memory of an old time
and the danger of the new.
We take our joy in small moments
                    small victories
                    small peacefulness
With grandchildren we are spared the old mistakes.
With our families we can be silent and say much.
With our friends we are strong enough to survive betrayal.
With the outside world we wear a different face.
With those who control our lives we are complacent
Giving rise to stories of our weakness.
What else is there to do?
We can no longer fight.
Even if we could, there is nothing left to win.
We say: Do not look too much ahead.
                    Do not look too far behind.
Be thankful for the sun that always comes up.
Be thankful for your blood that always flows.
This is the life we have to live now.
This is the way that chose us.

If I say yes to you,
you will say no to me.
If I give you all I have,
you will want what I do not own.
If I tell you I believe in mountains,
you will demand my true belief.
If I turn myself around for you,
you will want me lying down.
If I speak in the language you have taught me,
you will say I have forgotten my tongue.
If I live in the house you have built for me,
you will say I have forgotten my roots.
If I go to the school you insist is education,
you will blame me for learning too fast.
If I work at the job you say I should,
you will say I do work I should not.
If I tell you I must go my own way,
you will tell me it's the long way around.
If I acknowledge the friends that I have,
you will praise the ones I do not.
If I make something of myself,
you will want the other half.
If I am what I have become,
you will accept me for what I am not
And if what I am not is what you are,
Then I rejoice I am what I am.

Nachivera, wife of Chief Severo, 1894

All is a circle within me.
I am ten thousand winters old.
I am as young as a newborn flower.
I am a buffalo in its grave.
I am a tree in bloom.
All is a circle within me.
I have seen the world through an eagle's eyes
I have seen it from a gopher's hole.
I have seen the world on fire
And the sky without a moon.
All is a circle within me.
I have gone into the earth and out again.
I have gone to the edge of the sky.
Now all is at peace within me.
Now all has a place to come home.

Severo, chief of the Mouache band

Ah-ne-pitch, Tom-a-cita, and Ma-rez, 1899

Here on this mountain I am not alone
For all the lives I used to be are with me.
  I am the Last Great Warrior looking back
  At the white man beating paths
  Up our old game trails.
  I am the Last Young Brave chasing buffalo
  Putting his arrows away.
  I am the Last Young Maiden digging roots
  Leaving her reflection in the water.
  I am the Last Old Woman grinding corn
  Shedding her tears on the earth.
  I am the Last Great Chief standing tall
  Giving thanks for all our great hunts.
  I am the Buffalo, our Brother, and
  The Red-winged Blackbird, our Sister,
  Who have come to say good-by.
  I am the Rocks, the Trees, the River
  Who tell us not to cry.
  I go down the mountain with my people
  Taking away with us
  All we have left behind.
Here on this mountain I am not alone
For all the lives I used to be are with me.
All the lives tell me now I have come home.

The land I walk on is an ocean of concrete
Covering the paths my people used to take.
As I walk I hear the voices
Of my people in the earth.
I see the blood of my people
In every blade of grass.
I feel the spirit of my people
In the restless wind at night.
As I walk I hear my people.
They will come again.
You may build your world of broken glass
Make highways going backwards
Live in cities without a name
Plant the earth with plastic
Be at war with butterflies
In the end we will be waiting
In our homeland made of time.
In the end you will hear us coming
We are one footstep going on.

War Cry on a Prayer Feather was originally commissioned by the Colorado Council on the Arts and Humanities as a libretto, with music by Harold Farberman. It was presented by the Colorado Springs Symphony Orchestra as their Centennial/Bicentennial work and was nominated for a Pulitzer prize in music in 1977. In 1976, Nancy Wood also received a grant from the Colorado Centennial/Bicentennial Commission to photograph the rural people of the state for a year. The result was a traveling exhibition and a book, *The Grass Roots People: An American Requiem.* Ms. Wood, who came West from New Jersey in 1958, now lives in Ramah, Colorado, with her rancher husband, John Brittingham.